Animal MINIS!

What Kids Really Want to Know About Tiny Animals

by
cherie Winner

NORTHWORD
Minnetonka, Minnesota

Edited by Kristen McCurry
Designed by Lois A. Rainwater
Design concept by Michele Lanci-Altomare

Text © 2006 by Cherie Winner

NorthWord

Books for Young Readers
11571 K-Tel Drive
Minnetonka, MN 55343
www.tnkidsbooks.com

Photographs © 2006 provided by:

AAP/Paul Miller: p. 19 • AFP/AAP/Carl Bento: p. 33 • *Alamy Images:* Lisa Moore,
cover (shrew), p. 5; Scott Camazine, p. 17; Terry Fincher.Photo Int, p. 29 • *Animals
Animals-Earth Scenes:* Erwin & Peggy Bauer, cover (pygmy rabbit), p. 36;
Tim Shepherd/OSF, p. 43; David M. Dennis, pp. 47, 50 • Brand X: pp. 1 (bug), 26, 31, 57
(spider) • Corel: cover (flower), back cover (bug), p. 7 • Digital Vision:
pp. 48, 62 • Eyewire: back cover and p. 6 (hedgehog) • S. Blair Hedges, Ph.D.:
p. 22 • *istockphoto.com:* Tamara Bauer, p. 1 (dog); Maartje van Caspel, p. 27; Allen
Johnson, p. 51; Adrian Koeppel, p. 39 (top); Bruce MacQueen, pp. 1 (chickadee), 35;
Carolyn McKendry, pp. 54-55; Suzannah Skelton, p. 11; Mark Strevens, p. 52; Raymond
Truelove, p. 53 (chickadee); Scott Winegarden, p. 40; Lisa Young, p. 32 • *JupiterImages
Corporation:* pp. 3, 6 (lizard), 10, 37, 39 (bottom), 59 • Nathan Kley: p. 58
(snake) • *Minden Pictures:* Frans Lanting, p. 4; Mark Moffett, pp. 13 (ants), 21; Michael
Quinton, p. 44; Michael & Patricia Fogden, cover (hummingbird); Panda Photo/FLPA, p.
25 • Steve Winter/National Geographic Image Collection: p. 20 • Michael
Fairchild/Peter Arnold, Inc.: p. 14 • *Photo Researchers, Inc.:* Suzanne L. and Joseph
T. Collins, p. 58 (tortoise); Stephen Dalton, pp. 8-9; SPL, p. 16; Barbara Strnadova, cover
and p. 61 (butterfly); Merlin Tuttle, p. 24; Art Wolfe, p. 13 (bear) • PhotoDisc: back
cover (dog), pp. 1 (mouse), 15 (chicken), 28, 30, 53 (mouse) • *Punchstock.com:*
BananaStock, p. 57 (girl); Corbis, p. 45; PhotoDisc, p. 13 (lizard) • Michael Turco:
pp. 6 (frog), 60 • Two-Can Publishing (Simone End): p. 15 (illustration) • R. Behrstock/
VIREO: p. 23 • Rick and Nora Bowers/Visuals Unlimited: p. 61 (owl) • Gary Meszaros/
Visuals Unlimited: p. 41.

Library of Congress Cataloging-in-Publication Data

Winner, Cherie.
Animal minis! : what kids really want to know about tiny animals /
by Cherie Winner.
p. cm. -- (Kids' faqs)
Includes bibliographical references (p. 62).
ISBN 1-55971-933-8 (hardcover) -- ISBN 1-55971-934-6 (softcover)
1. Animals--Juvenile literature. I. Title. II. Series.

QL49.W563 2006
590--dc22   2005018641

Printed in Singapore
10 9 8 7 6 5 4 3 2 1

Acknowledgments

The author thanks Steven D. Werman, Ph.D., of Mesa State College, and George Callison, Ph.D., for sharing their stories about mini critters.

Dedication

To the 4th-grade students and teachers at Shelledy School in Fruita, Colorado, for inviting me into their classes

—C.W.

contents

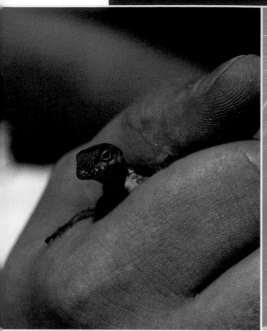

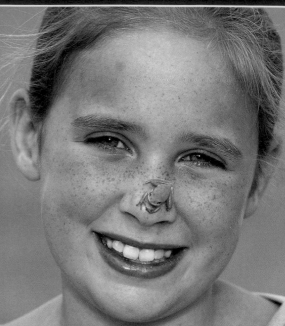

Lizards, frogs, and hedgehogs
are just a few of the critters that come
in extra-small sizes.

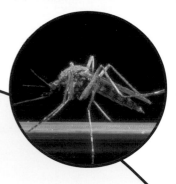

introduction

"BIGGER IS BETTER." HAVE YOU HEARD THAT SAYING BEFORE? DO YOU THINK IT'S TRUE?

Maybe it's true if we're talking about pizzas or football players. But what about animals? Some young friends and I got to thinking about all the animals we see that are smaller than we are, like bugs, mice, frogs, and birds. So we wondered: if bigger really is better, why are there so many small animals around? If you add up all the tiny animals out there, they outnumber bigger animals like us thousands to one! Could there be something good about being small?

Little creatures do have certain advantages. They can do all sorts of things bigger animals can't. A shrew can hide under a single maple leaf, and a mosquito can fly through a ripped screen door as it's chasing after a meal (you!).

Of course, there are problems, too. For one thing, tiny animals have a hard time staying warm—they're too small to carry around a heavy fur coat! For another, they must constantly be on the lookout for food. People use the phrase "eats like a bird" to mean someone who doesn't eat much, but a person who really ate like a bird might scarf down his own weight in food every day.

Mostly, being small is just different. Luckily animals probably don't spend too much time wishing they were a different size. However, if you've ever seen a tiny lizard dart up a wall as if gravity didn't exist, it's easy to see why, for some, "Smaller is better!"

Why does being small help a lizard climb a wall?

They're light enough that they can use friction to cling to the wall. They have zillions of tiny flaps on their toes, something like your fingerprints. If you move your fingertips along a smooth surface, you can feel the friction that pulls against your movement. It's as if the ridges on your fingers

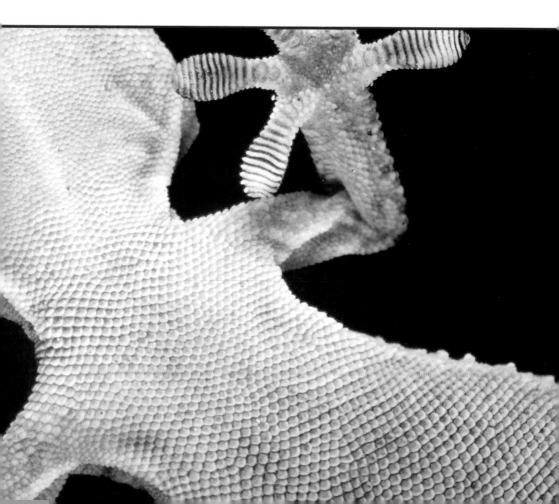

grab onto the surface a little bit. Now imagine that the ridges on your fingertips have even tinier ridges that can only be seen with a microscope. Small lizards weigh so little, and they have so many ridges on their toes, that the ridges can support their whole weight.

Even if they fall when they're climbing, small lizards usually don't hit the ground hard enough to hurt themselves. Gravity doesn't affect lightweight animals as much as it does heavier animals.

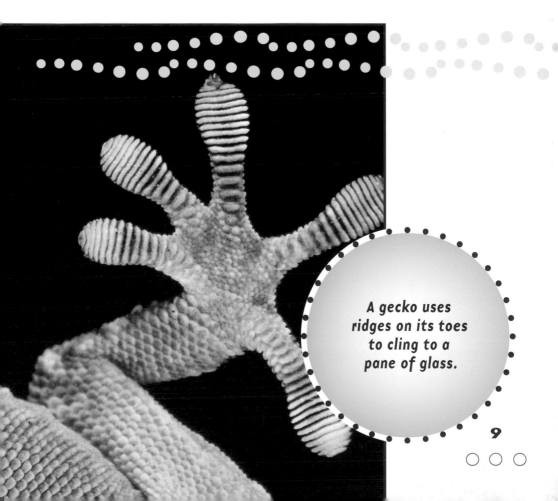

A gecko uses ridges on its toes to cling to a pane of glass.

Isn't gravity the same for all animals?

Gravity is the same, meaning it pulls things down with the same force, no matter how big or small. But how much we feel it depends on how big we are. Lighter creatures feel it less than heavier creatures. A few years ago, a team of scientists

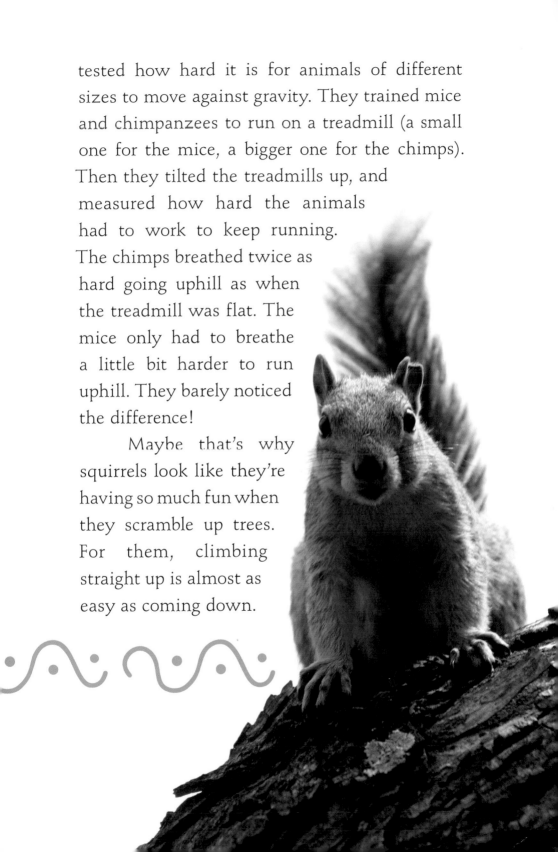

tested how hard it is for animals of different sizes to move against gravity. They trained mice and chimpanzees to run on a treadmill (a small one for the mice, a bigger one for the chimps). Then they tilted the treadmills up, and measured how hard the animals had to work to keep running. The chimps breathed twice as hard going uphill as when the treadmill was flat. The mice only had to breathe a little bit harder to run uphill. They barely noticed the difference!

Maybe that's why squirrels look like they're having so much fun when they scramble up trees. For them, climbing straight up is almost as easy as coming down.

How many kinds of mini animals are there?

It depends on what we count as a "mini" animal. Almost all the mammals, birds, reptiles, amphibians, and fishes, plus all 750,000 kinds of insects, are smaller than we are.

Some animals are as big as we are or even bigger, but small compared to their close relatives. The Malayan sun bear weighs up to 145 pounds (66 kg)—bigger than you, probably, but a lot smaller than other kinds of bears. Then there's the pygmy hippopotamus, which can weigh more than 500 pounds (227 kg). That doesn't sound "mini" at all! But other hippos grow to ten times that size. In the hippo world, pygmy hippos are definitely mini.

Even among true minis, there's a big range in size. Ants, for instance, are a lot smaller than we are, but the smallest ones are 40 times smaller than the biggest ones. Even to other ants, these ants look tiny. In human terms, that would be like having people who are only 2 inches (5 cm) tall. (Watch where you step!)

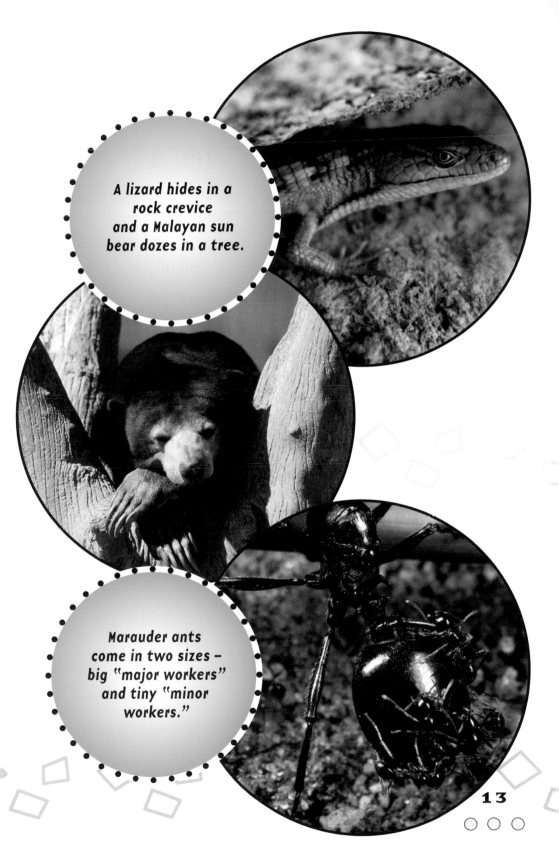

A lizard hides in a rock crevice and a Malayan sun bear dozes in a tree.

Marauder ants come in two sizes – big "major workers" and tiny "minor workers."

13

What's the most unusual miniature animal?

Maybe the prize for weirdest small animal goes to the paradoxical frog of South America. It's about 2 inches (5 cm) long. That may not be unusual for a frog, but what is unusual is that the tadpole it developed from was much

A pygmy hippo mother protects her baby, which is barely as tall as the grass.

larger: up to 10 inches (25 cm) long! When the tadpole became a frog, it shrank to a fifth of its former size. Now that's weird.

Personally, I like the small animals that I expected to be bigger, like the Malayan sun bear and pygmy hippo. Even dinosaurs came in extra-small sizes. During the last few years, archaeologists have found fossil dinosaurs that were only about the size of a modern-day chicken!

What's the smallest insect?

Nobody knows. There are many kinds of insects that you can barely see without a magnifying glass. They weigh about as much as a speck of dust. In fact, next time you see bits of dust floating in a sunbeam, take a closer look. Some of those floating bits are actually teeny-tiny insects.

In real life, this parasitic wasp is smaller than one of the dots around this circle. A different wasp laid her eggs on a caterpillar (next page).

Some of the smallest insects are parasitic wasps. They look like the big wasps you might see hovering around a spilled soda in the park, but they are about 10,000 times smaller. They are called "parasitic" because they feed off of another live animal. Female parasitic wasps lay their eggs on caterpillars. Some actually poke the caterpillar with a needle-like structure, and lay their eggs inside the caterpillar. When the baby wasps hatch out, they eat the caterpillar. It's a great strategy for the wasps because the babies don't have to search for food. But it's definitely bad news for the caterpillar!

What's the smallest fish?

For a long time, the dwarf goby held the record as the smallest fish in the world. It even made it into the *Guinness Book of World Records*. Dwarf gobies are only about a third of an inch (8.5 mm) long. That's about one third as long as a small goldfish. Dwarf gobies live along coral reefs near Japan and the Philippines.

Then in 2004, scientists announced that they had found a species of fish that's even smaller. The stout infantfish is a bit shorter than the dwarf goby, and even though it is called "stout," it is thinner than the dwarf goby. It lives along coral reefs near Australia.

The stout infantfish is not only the smallest fish. It's also the smallest vertebrate, or animal with a backbone. That means it's smaller than any other fish, amphibian, reptile, bird, or mammal on Earth. That is, unless someone finds another species that is even smaller.

Believe it or not, this squiggly thing is a full-grown stout infantfish.

What's the smallest amphibian?

It's a close contest. The Habana robber frog and Monte Iberia eleuth from Cuba are just 0.3 to 0.5 inch (8.5 to 12.7 mm) long (with their hind legs tucked in). That's a tiny bit tinier than the gold frog from Brazil. All three kinds of frogs live in lush forests and eat very small insects. A salamander from Mexico called Thorius is also in the running. It's about 0.7 of an inch (1.8 cm) long and very slender. It weighs about the same as one of the littlest frogs.

They look like toys, but they're real live frogs: the Habana robber frog (right) and gold frog (next page).

What's the smallest reptile?

This is another close contest. In fact, it's too close to call. Two kinds of lizards called the Monito gecko and the Jaragua gecko win the prize as smallest reptile. Each is just 1.3 inches (3.3 cm) long, including the tail. That's about half the length of a toothpick. Each species lives on a different island in the Caribbean Sea. They were discovered just a few years ago and are very rare.

What's the smallest bird?

All hummingbirds are small, but the bee hummingbirds that live in Cuba are the smallest of all. They got their name because you might think they were big bees if you saw or heard them buzz by. They're only about 2.25 inches (5.7 cm) long and weigh eight one-hundredths of an ounce (2.3 g)–less than a penny! Most hummingbirds are at least twice that size.

Bee hummingbirds can beat their tiny wings 70 times per second. That's three times faster than medium-sized hummingbirds.

These amazing little birds are endangered. Many of the forests they live in have been cleared for farming and for lumber.

What's the smallest mammal?

The bumblebee bat is the shortest, and the Etruscan shrew weighs the least.

A bumblebee bat is so small, it can fit on the tip of a man's thumb. It weighs six to seven one-hundredths of an ounce (1.7 to 2 g). That's about the same as a paper clip. These bats are so light they can hover in midair, like hummingbirds. Most bats are too big to do that. Bumblebee bats were first discovered in 1974, in caves along a river in Thailand. They are one of the most endangered species on Earth.

Shrews look like long-nosed mice, but they aren't rodents. They belong to a group of animals called insectivores. They eat spiders, insects, and worms. Most shrews are about twice as big as the Etruscan shrew, whose head and body together are 1.4 to 2 inches (3.6 to 5 cm) long. Its tail is about an inch (2.5 cm) long. Some Etruscan shrews are real porkers, weighing nearly one-tenth of an ounce (2.5 g), but others only reach half that size. That's why they are counted as one of the smallest mammals. Despite their size, they are fierce hunters that often kill and eat prey animals that are bigger than they are. They live along the coast of the Mediterranean Sea.

Between hunting trips, an Etruscan shrew naps on a bed of moss.

It sounds like a lot of the smallest animals weren't discovered until just a few years ago. Why did it take us so long to find them?

Mini animals are harder to find than bigger ones. They're so small they can be hard to see. They often live in out-of-the-way places such as under leaves or in burrows. Even if you do see one, you might not be able to catch it because tiny animals scurry out of reach so quickly. If you're a biologist trying to figure out if a critter belongs to a new, extra-small species, you have to catch more than one. You need to find several members of the same species before you can say for sure that the species is smaller than its relatives.

A magnifying lens or microscope reveals a whole world of mini critters.

Another thing you might have noticed from our list of smallest critters is that many of them are rare or endangered. Their habitats are being destroyed. So these smallest animals are hard to find, hard to catch, and there aren't many around. No wonder it has taken us so long to find them and learn about them. Maybe there are other tiny critters yet to be discovered!

Why are there so many different names for mini animals, like "pygmy" or "dwarf"?

Pygmy is a name for a kind of animal that is smaller than its close relatives, such as pygmy rabbits and pygmy hippopotamuses. Both are about half the size of other kinds of rabbits and hippos. Sometimes "midget" is used instead of "pygmy," as it is in the name of the midget faded rattlesnake. It's also a rude word for a very small person.

The words miniature and dwarf are sometimes used as if they mean the same thing. Other times, they mean

Cardigan Welsh corgi, a true dwarf among dogs

something different about how the animal looks. A miniature looks like its full-sized cousins, only smaller. But a dwarf has different proportions than a normal-sized animal. Usually their legs are shorter and stockier. You can see dwarfs and miniatures in the dog world. Welsh corgis are dwarfs. Their legs are much shorter than you'd expect from the size of their torso and head. Miniature poodles look like "standard" poodles, except that they're smaller.

Horses are bigger than dogs, right?
Not if the horse is a Falabella and the dog is a Great Dane.

Could there ever be a bird or a mammal the size of a bug?

Probably not. Scientists think the bee hummingbird, Etruscan shrew, and bumblebee bat are about as mini as a bird or mammal can be. The problem with getting smaller is that their heart couldn't beat fast enough to keep their body supplied with oxygen.

Compared to their size, little birds and mammals use a lot more oxygen than big ones. That's because they lose heat more quickly from their tiny bodies, and they have to have a faster metabolism in order to stay warm. That means they have to breathe faster to bring in more oxygen. Their hearts have to work hard to pump that oxygen to all the organs, through the blood stream. When a shrew or hummingbird is resting, its heart pumps about 600 times every minute. When the animal is active, its heart pumps even harder—nearly 1300 times every minute! If the animal were any smaller, its heart would have to work even faster. But it can't. It's already going as fast as it can.

Then why can insects be so much smaller?

Insects can be smaller because they use a completely different way to get oxygen to all parts of the body. Oxygen isn't carried by their blood. Instead, tiny tubes carry oxygen directly from the air through the whole body.

This is a great system for very tiny animals. It doesn't work in bigger animals, though. (Lucky for us, or we might be surrounded by insects the size of elephants.)

Ants can't be our size, and we can't be their size.

Do mini animals have all the same parts bigger animals have?

The quick answer is yes. All animals must have the parts that will let them navigate in their world, get food, stay safe, find a mate, and raise offspring. Most shrews, for instance, have 32 teeth, the same number as adult humans.

But with some body parts, tiny animals can get by with fewer parts than big animals have. In dogs, the number of toes can depend on the size of the dog. Tiny dogs such as Chihuahuas sometimes have fewer toes, and giant dogs such as Great Danes sometimes have extra toes.

Then there's the stout infantfish, the tiniest fish in the world. It is so tiny that it almost doesn't look like a fish. Instead of a fin on its back, it has a few stubby spikes. It has big eyes, gills, a gut, and a reproductive system. No bright colors, big fins, or fancy shapes. Just the basics.

Some tiny animals can get by with fewer body parts than bigger animals.

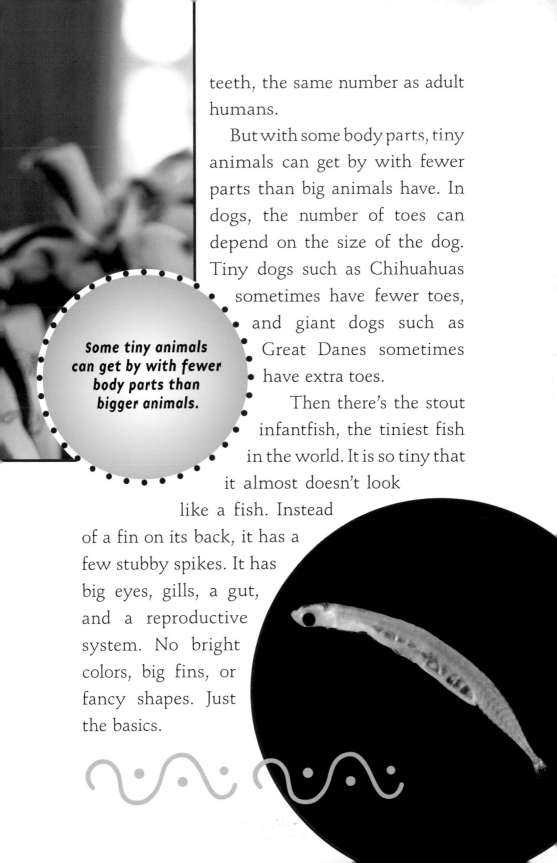

Are mini animals as smart as bigger ones?
How big are their brains?

Their brains are very small, but tiny animals are still smart enough to do all the things they need to do to survive. They can hear, see, taste, hunt, hide, communicate with others of their kind, and raise families just as well as big animals can. Some of them can even do things we can't, like hear high sounds and sense when a big storm is coming.

Do mini animals make mini sounds?
Can they hear us?

Small animals can be very noisy. Chickadees are known for their chatter, and mice and shrews make high, shrill whistles. Some of the sounds they make are pitched so high we can't hear them. Our ears are too far apart! In order to hear very high sounds, the ears must be close together. Since small animals have ears that are closer together than ours, they can hear higher sounds than we can. They can hear us, but we can't always hear them.

Small size doesn't mean small sounds!

Where can I look for mini animals?

Your home is probably surrounded by minis! Ask your local park naturalist or your state's Game & Fish Department about the kinds of tiny animals that live in your area, and how you can get a peek at them in their natural habitat.

If you want to see the bee hummingbird or the Habana robber frog, you'll have to go to

Cuba, but other small hummingbirds and frogs live throughout North America. So do shrews, lizards, bats, and minnows. If you live in Oregon or Idaho, you might even catch a glimpse of a pygmy rabbit, which is so little it looks almost like a baby bunny of some other species.

And if you live on an island, you're really in luck. Islands are the best places of all to look for animal minis.

They look like babies, but this pygmy rabbit and these minnows are all grown up.

Why do islands have so many mini animals?

Islands are special places. The only animals that live there naturally are those whose ancestors were able to swim, fly, or float across miles of open water. As a result, islands usually don't have as many different species as the mainland. That makes life on an island very different.

Island animals might have less food (either plants or animals) than they would on the mainland. But they also might not have as many predators or as many other animals to compete with for the same foods. Either way, being a lot smaller or a lot bigger could be an advantage.

Over time some species became very large because they had few predators on the island and no longer had to be small enough to hide. Other species got smaller over time because their food was scarce on the island and only small animals could find enough food to survive. Today, islands are home to both the biggest and the smallest members of many animal groups.

These ocean islands might be home to mini critters—or to animal giants.

A hummingbird
drinks nectar
and a shrew chomps
a centipede.

What do mini animals eat?

Mini animals eat everything bigger animals eat, just in smaller bites. Some are herbivores, or plant-eaters. Others are carnivores, or meat-eaters. Shrews are a special kind of carnivore called an insectivore, or insect-eater. They catch and eat insects and worms. Many small animals will eat both plants and animals, depending on what they find. Hummingbirds pluck insects from the same flowers they visit to get nectar. They can even nab insects in midair.

Tiny animals don't eat much, do they?

Actually, tiny animals eat a lot more than larger animals do, relative to their size. If you weighed everything a pygmy shrew eats in one day, you'd find it doesn't weigh much at all. But compared to the size of the shrew, it's a huge amount. A pygmy shrew eats almost the whole time it's awake. It chows down at least twice its own weight in food every day!

Imagine doing the same thing yourself. You could sit on one end of a seesaw while a friend stacks burgers, pizza, and ice cream on the other end. When the seesaw balances, the food on the other end weighs the same as you. That's only half of what you'll eat today! Do the same thing tomorrow, and the next day, and every day after that. Do you feel full yet?

A pygmy shrew
can eat a big,
fat earthworm
in one day.

So, why do tiny animals eat so much?

Tiny mammals and birds need to eat a lot to stay warm. All mammals and birds generate their own heat by using food as fuel. Little bodies cool off faster than big bodies do, so small animals have to "burn" more food to keep their body temperature where it should be. They also can't carry as much fat, fur, or feathers as insulation.

Do mini animals poop?

Sure they do. Every animal makes wastes that come out as solid (feces) or liquid (urine). Small animals just make smaller amounts of waste than big animals do. A pygmy shrew makes droppings that look like a half a grain of rice, and releases about one drop of urine when it urinates. Even tinier animals make even smaller amounts of waste. Fly poop looks like specks of dust. And you might need a microscope to see the poop of parasitic wasps!

How do mini animals keep from being eaten by bigger animals?

Small animals have many ways of staying safe. They can be hard to find. They are small enough to slip into hidey-holes where larger predators can't follow, and quick enough to get there before the predator catches up with them.

Some, like shrews, are fierce fighters. Any predator that tries to kill a shrew will probably get bitten. And if a predator does manage to chomp down on a shrew, it will get a nasty surprise. Shrews taste awful. (Or so I've heard—I've never tasted one myself!)

The midget faded rattlesnake makes up for its miniature size with an especially deadly kind of venom. Other rattlesnakes can grow to 7 feet (214 cm) or longer, but the midget faded rattler only reaches about 2 feet (61 cm) long. Young rattlesnakes of all kinds make a more toxic venom than adults do. As they grow up, other rattlers switch to the milder adult venom. Midget faded rattlers don't switch. They make the stronger venom their whole lives.

Small but deadly, a midget faded rattlesnake packs a big punch.

Do small animals ever gang up on bigger ones?

Yes! If a hawk or owl comes near their nests, small birds like chickadees, wrens, and warblers will gang up on it. They scold the intruder. They peck at its tail. They dive-bomb it from above. This is called mobbing. It lets

The delicate dik-dik fakes out predators with big piles of poop.

all the birds in the neighborhood know the predator is there. The hawk or owl could kill them easily—if it could catch them. But the little birds are quicker and more agile than the bigger bird. They rarely get caught. Sometimes they even chase the predator away.

Some mini animals puff up their fur or fluff out their feathers to try to look bigger than they really are. Then there are the dik-diks. These little antelope have a totally different way to fake out predators. Most of the antelope that roam in Africa are the size of a deer, or bigger. But dik-diks only stand 14 to 16 inches (35.6 to 40.6 cm) tall at the shoulder. That's about to the top of your knees. Dik-diks live in pairs or small family groups. Each group claims its territory by pooping at certain places along the borders. Every member of the group poops in the same spots. If you saw a dik-dik poop pile, you'd think it was made by a large antelope. You wouldn't know it was made by several very small antelope. Sometimes dik-diks even poop on top of dung left by other animals—including elephants! Potential predators might take one look at such a pile and decide to look elsewhere for an easy lunch.

Tiny, medium,
and extra-large:
eggs of a
hummingbird, chicken,
and ostrich.

How tiny are the babies of tiny animals?

Babies of tiny animals are much bigger, compared to their parents, than babies of big animals. An ostrich mother weighs 100 times as much as her egg, which is the size of a soccer ball. But a hummingbird mother weighs only 10 times as much as her egg, which is the size of a jellybean. Tiny moms have it tough— making a baby that's one-tenth your size is a lot more work than making a baby that's one-hundredth your size!

Baby hummingbirds wait for their mom in their tiny nest.

Do mini animals live as long as bigger ones?

Mini animals don't live as many years as bigger animals. But if you count how many times an animal's heart beats in a lifetime, you find something amazing.

Almost all mammals, of every size, live for 800 million to one billion heartbeats. Then they die. Scientists think that because everything works faster in small animals—their heart, lungs,

An eagle lives longer than a chickadee, and a chickadee lives about twice as long as a mouse of the same size.

and other organs—small animals wear out quicker. A mouse's heart beats about 600 times every minute. It reaches 800 million heartbeats in just 3 years. An elephant's heart beats 30 times a minute—and lasts about 50 years.

Those are "normal" life spans for mice and elephants. Some individuals die much sooner, because they get sick or a predator kills them. Some live longer, because they manage to escape the dangers usually faced by members of their species.

With humans, it's different. We are mammals like mice and elephants, but we live for about 3 billion heartbeats. Scientists aren't sure why.

Birds live longer than mammals of the same size. However, just as with mammals, larger species of birds live longer than smaller ones.

How far can mini animals travel?

Most minis don't travel very far. They find everything they need in a small area. There are a few exceptions, though. Many of the

hummingbirds that we see in North America in summer migrate to Central or South America for the winter. They fly hundreds or thousands of miles every fall, and then fly back again in spring. Most fly over land, so they can stop and refuel during the trip, but ruby-throated hummingbirds cross the entire Gulf of Mexico without stopping.

A hummingbird sips from spring flowers after its long journey north.

Could we ever shrink ourselves to the size of a mouse or even smaller?

Unfortunately, we can't have the kinds of adventures shown in movies like *The Borrowers, Fantastic Voyage,* and *Honey, I Shrunk the Kids.* If we did find a way to shrink ourselves to the size of mice, our hearts would race and we'd be breathing so fast we wouldn't be able to do much else. We might try to talk, but we probably wouldn't be able to understand each other because our voices would come out too squeaky.

It's fun to imagine being tiny, though. You could slip under doors into locked rooms, nibble cookie crumbs the size of layer cakes, and make a cozy bed out of lint. Of course, it might be scary to come face-to-face with a spider or a cockroach that is as big as you are!

There could be other problems, too. It's amazing that many mini animals are in danger of becoming extinct. After all, they don't eat much and they don't take up much space. But they do need certain things, or they can't survive. For example, a bee hummingbird must find the right kind of flowers to sip from, and a stout infantfish will die if the coral reefs it lives in are destroyed. Sometimes when we think of conservation and helping endangered species we only think about big animals. But little critters deserve help, too.

The world would look very different if you were a teeny-tiny lizard or an insect no bigger than a speck of dust. But "different" can be OK. For most of the animals on Earth, being small is just right.

Thread snake

Southern speckled padloper

A thread snake snacks on a tiny ant pupa, and the world's smallest turtle species hides among some leaves.

more "smallests"

Smallest snake

Thread snakes live in many parts of the world. Sometimes they are called worm snakes, but they are even smaller than many worms. A thread snake is about the same diameter as the tips of your shoelaces.

Smallest turtle or tortoise

The southern speckled padloper from South Africa is 2.4 to 4.3 inches (6.1 to 10.9 cm) long when it's fully grown. It looks a bit like a Galapagos tortoise, but is even smaller than its big cousin's head.

Smallest hoofed animal

The dwarf royal antelope is only 10 to 12 inches (25 to 30 cm) tall at the shoulder and weighs 4.4 to 6.6 pounds (2 to 3 kg). Its African name means "king of the rabbits."

Smallest monkey

The pygmy marmoset is about 6 inches (15.2 cm) long (not counting the tail) and weighs no more than 8 ounces (.2 kg). That's between the size of a chipmunk and a tree squirrel. It ducks behind leaves to hide from the predators that prowl the jungles of South America.

Pygmy marmoset

Smallest shark

Under a magnifying glass, the dwarf lantern shark looks as fierce as any other shark. But it's only 6 to 8 inches (15.2 to 20.3 cm) long! It lives in deep parts of the Caribbean Sea.

Western pygmy blue

Smallest butterfly

Even when its wings are spread wide open, the western pygmy blue is just 0.7 inch (1.8 cm) across. It flits among flowers in the southwestern United States.

Smallest owl

The elf owl is 5.75 inches (14.6 cm) long and weighs 1.4 ounces (39.7 g). That's only about half the size of a robin. Elf owls live in Mexico and the southwestern United States.

Elf owl

resources

BOOKS

CALDER, WILLIAM A. *Size, Function, and Life History.* Cambridge, MA: Harvard University Press, 1984.

EVANS, HOWARD ENSIGN. *Life on a Little-Known Planet.* New York: Dutton, 1993.

SCHMIDT-NIELSEN, KNUT. *How Animals Work.* New York: Cambridge University Press, 1993 (1972).

SCHMIDT-NIELSEN, KNUT. *Scaling: Why Is Animal Size So Important?* New York: Cambridge University Press, 1984.

SIBLEY, DAVID ALLEN. *The Sibley Guide to Bird Life and Behavior.* New York: Alfred A. Knopf, 2001.

SIBLEY, DAVID ALLEN. *The Sibley Guide to Birds.* New York: Alfred A. Knopf, 2000.

STONE, RICHARD. *Mammoth: The Resurrection of an Ice Age Giant.* Cambridge, MA: Perseus Publishing, 2001.

VOTAW, Melanie. *Hummingbirds: Jewels on Air.* Philadelphia: Running Press Book Publishers, 2003.

WEB SITES

www.42explore.com/ants.htm
This site has lots of info on ants and a great list of links you can follow to learn more about all kinds of insects.

www.enchantedlearning.com/subjects/butterfly/allabout/extremes.shtml
If you like butterflies and want to know the smallest, biggest, fastest, slowest, and more, this is the page for you.

**www.enchantedlearning.com/subjects/dinosaurs/
dinos/Compy.shtml**
Here's another great page from Enchanted Learning. This one gives you
the lowdown on a very small dinosaur known as Compsognathus.

www.didyouknow.cd/animals/frogs.htm
Go to this site to read about the world's smallest (and biggest) frogs and
see amazing photos of both.

www.pbs.org/wnet/nature/cuba/eco_explorer4.html
See Cuba's special small animals—tiny frogs, a butterfly bat, and the bee
hummingbird. Follow the link to a page of wildlife photos you can send
as e-cards.

http://allaboutfrogs.org/weird/strange/small.html
This page features great photos of three of the smallest frogs on Earth,
with a coin and a person's hand for comparison.

www.flmnh.ufl.edu/fish/education/questions/Basics.html
This web site from the University of Florida's Museum of Natural
History tells you everything you always wanted to know about small
sharks (and big ones, too!).

www.nps.gov/chis/pygmy.htm
Find out about a prehistoric mini: the pygmy mammoth once roamed
southern California. This site from Channel Islands National Park
includes photos of a fossilized mammoth that's no taller than a man.

www.zoo.org/educate/fact_sheets/sun_bear/sbear.htm
Seattle's Woodland Park Zoo offers this site about Malayan sun bears,
the smallest bears in the world.

www.zoo.org/educate/fact_sheets/marmoset/marmoset.htm
While you're at the Woodland Park Zoo web site, surf on over to this
page about the world's smallest monkey. You'll find loads of cool
information about their family life, how they communicate, and what
they think makes a great snack.

www.owling.com/Elf.htm
This site not only shows pictures of elf owls and tells about their life, it
also features recordings of elf owls calling at night.

About the Author

CHERIE WINNER is a science writer for Washington State University and also writes books and articles for children and adults. Her favorite subjects are animals and plants, and the people who study them. Several of her books have been named Outstanding Science Trade Books for Children. Dr. Winner has taught college classes, done research on salamanders, and worked as a newspaper reporter. Nowadays, when she isn't writing about nature, she enjoys creating mini-habitats to attract mini critters to her yard in Pullman, Washington.

Do you have questions about other animals? We want to hear from you! E-mail us at **kidsfaqs@tnkidsbooks.com**. For more details, log on to **www.tnkidsbooks.com**.